Wolfgang Amadeus MOZART

CONCERTO

in

G MAJOR

for

PIANO

and

ORCHESTRA

KV453

MUSIC MINUS ONE

SUGGESTIONS FOR USING THIS MMO EDITION

WE HAVE TRIED to create a product that will provide you an easy way to learn and perform this concerto with a full orchestra in the comfort of your own home. Because it involves a fixed orchestral performance, there is an inherent lack of flexibility in tempo and cadenza length. The following MMO features and techniques will reduce these inflexibilities and help you maximize the effectiveness of the MMO practice and performance system:

Where the soloist begins a movement *solo*, we have provided an introductory measure with subtle taps inserted at the actual tempo before the soloist's entrance. Taps have also been inserted in the recording where they aid in synchronizing with an orchestra entrance, e.g., with a tempo change. These taps are inserted in the right channel only and can be reduced or amplified by adjusting your balance control.

Chapter stops on your CD are conveniently located throughout the piece at the beginnings of practice sections, and are cross-referenced in the score. This should help you quickly find a desired place in the music as you learn the piece.

Chapter stops have also been placed at orchestra entrances (e.g., after cadenzas) so that, with the help of a second person, it is possible to perform a seamless version of the concerto alongside your MMO CD accompaniment. While we have allotted what is generally considered an average amount of time for a cadenza,

each performer will have a different interpretation (or in some cases substitute a different cadenza) and observe individual tempi. Your personal rendition may preclude a perfect "fit" within the space provided. Therefore, by having a second person press the pause ❙❙ button on your CD player after the start of each cadenza, followed by the next track ▶▶❙ button, your CD will be cued to the orchestra's re-entry. When you as soloist are at the end of the cadenza or other solo passage, the second person can press the play ▶ (or pause ❙❙ button) on the CD remote to allow a synchronized orchestra re-entry.

We have observed generally accepted tempi, but some may wish to perform at a different tempo, or to slow down or speed up the accompaniment for practice purposes. In addition to the practice version included with this edition (see below), you can purchase from MMO (or from other audio and electronics dealers) specialized CD players & recorders which allow variable speed while maintaining proper pitch. This is an indispensable tool for the serious musician and you may wish to look into purchasing this useful piece of equipment for full enjoyment of all your MMO editions.

We want to provide you with the most useful practice and performance accompaniments possible. If you have any suggestions for improving the MMO system, please feel free to contact us. You can reach us by e-mail at *info@musicminusone.com*.

ABOUT THE 'PRACTICE TEMPO' VERSION

As an aid during the early stages of learning this concerto, we have included a second compact disc with the same layout as the 'A' disc, containing the complete reference version of the concerto repeated at full speed, followed by a special 'practice tempo' accompaniment recording that has been slowed by approximately 20%. This will allow you to begin at a comfortably reduced speed until fingerings and technique are more firmly in grasp, at which time the full-speed accompaniment can be substituted.

3085

Contents

MOZART'S PIANO CONCERTO IN G MAJOR, KV453

This great concerto, once overshadowed by the (other) great concerti by Mozart, e.g. KV466, 467, 488, has been rediscovered, both as a "teaching" piece as well as a performable work. It is not the most lyrically memorable of Mozart's concerti, nor is it among the most brilliant; however, the slow movement ranks high on the list of works of tender sentiment, and it is by no means a piece without technical pitfalls. The G-major Concerto is a masterpiece, composed in the greatest of composer's mature years. It demands careful study.

In regard to tempo, I have heard the opening allegro performed as slow as quarter note =116 and as fast as 144+. For me, a tempo between 132 and 138 feels best, depending upon the piano, hall, etc. For this recording, I stayed close to 132. The Andante can be a problem; guard against a divided beat on the one hand, and too sprightly thirty seconds on the other. There is much sadness in this profoundly beautiful movement. The last movement is really problematic in terms of speed. The half-note=80 is the most commonly used tempo and seems about right, but the theme can sound a bit stodgy at this speed if the character and touch are not perfect. On the other hand, this tempo feels like a presto when applied to the variation beginning at bar 72 in the piano (65 in the orchestra). Many players take a somewhat slower tempo from bar 65 until measure 128 (half note=72/76) and resume Tempo I at the return to G Major (or even a bit faster than tempo!). Claude Frank advises this in his open rehearsal video entitled Concerto! (This is an interesting production, by the way, and I would recommend it to students of KV453.) The coda is to be played *quasi doppio movimento* in my view, which is not so easy to do! Played on the typical Steinway, these tempi seem to work best. I prefer to play Mozart on a lighter actioned and toned instrument, like a fine Bechstein or Bosendorfer, in which case brisker tempi feel right:

Included in the following edition are my suggestions for fingering solutions and thoughts about ornamentation realizations and questionable notes. Of course, other editions should always be consulted and decisions made by the individual performer based upon his or her own best judgment.

—*Paul Van Ness*

CONCERTO № 17
for
PIANO *and* ORCHESTRA
G major 𝄵 G-dur

KV453

Wolfgang Amadeus Mozart
(1756-1791)

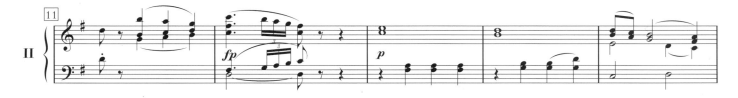

6

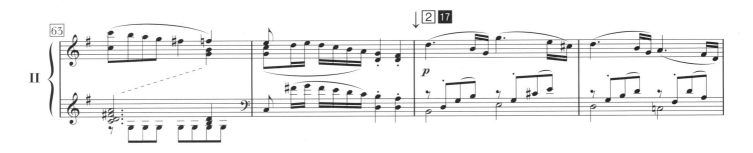

Bar 75 ornament (tr): I play this as four sixteenth-notes, starting on the principal note., This makes the orchestra at bar 78 a commentary on the theme, as I am sure it was intended. Most pianists begin on the auxiliary (c) and add the suffix. It spoils the effect in my view (Leonard Bernstein concurred). Likewise, if you look at the fourth beat of bar 98, the piano and orchestra must conform. Here, the piano starts on the auxiliary, not because of any rule that states it must, but because it sounds better to have four sixteenths than five at this point. In other words, it is a matter of taste and good sense, not rules and regulations!

Bar 76: The legato marked for the bass is probably not Mozart's. I take this from Paul Badura-Skoda's comments in his book. The orchestral theme is accompanied staccato, so you can choose which feels better. I have played it both ways.

Bars 87-88: There are no slurs in the score and I prefer to play these lightly detached and rhythmically alert. Generally, I observe the articulations in the Eulenberg pocket score over any piano score. I think that later editors placed too much emphasis on legato, thereby adding slurs where not necessary. That is not to say that I like chopped-up phrases, but simply that composers of Mozart's day attached a different significance to articulation than musicians of later generations.

10

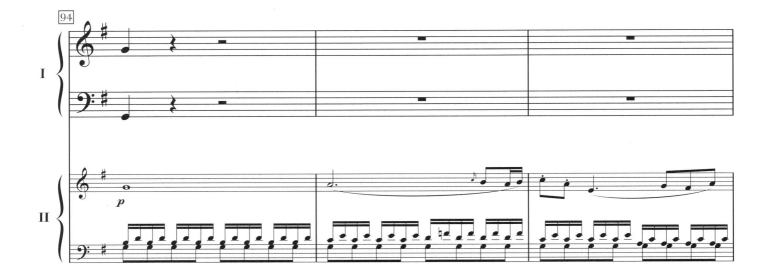

MMO 3085

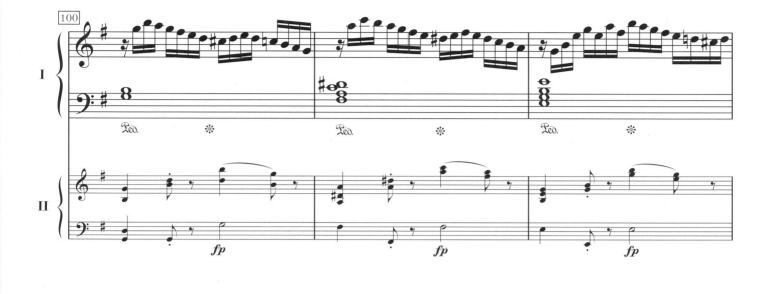

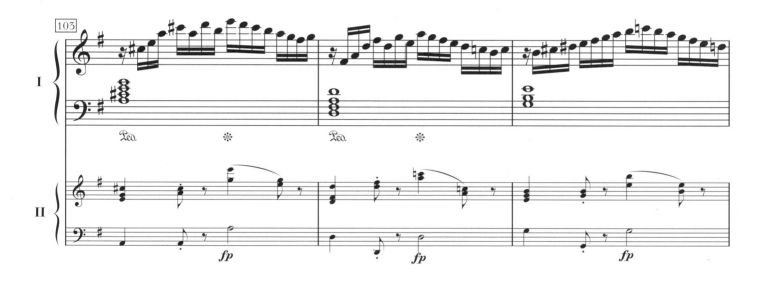

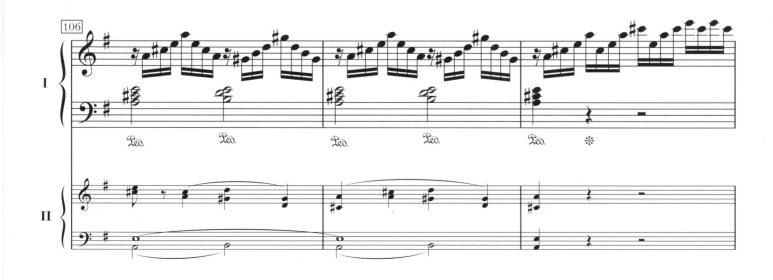

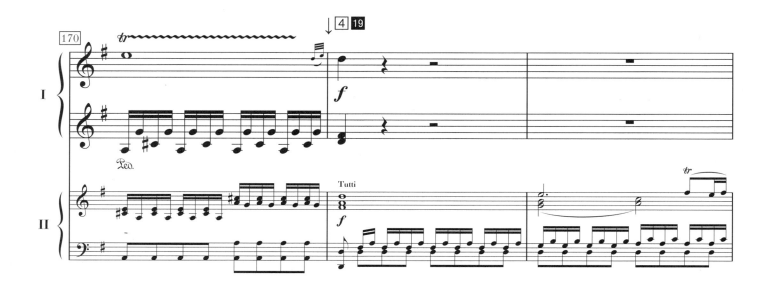

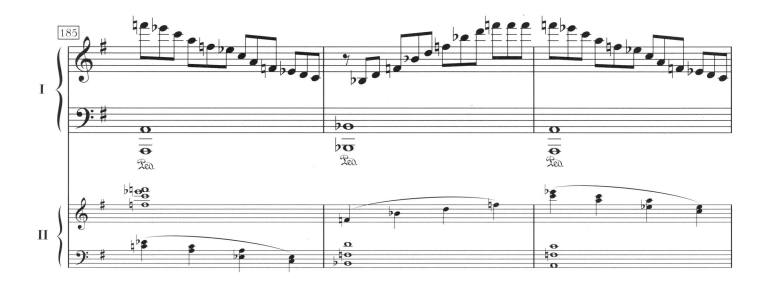

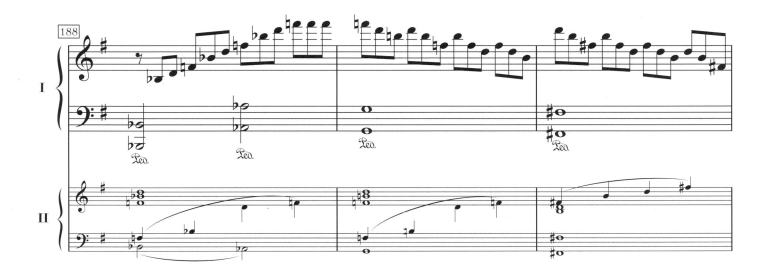

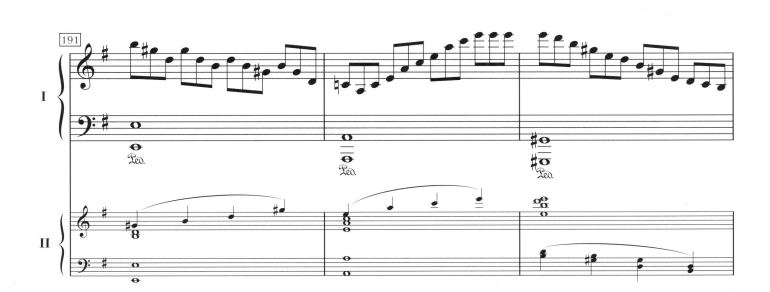

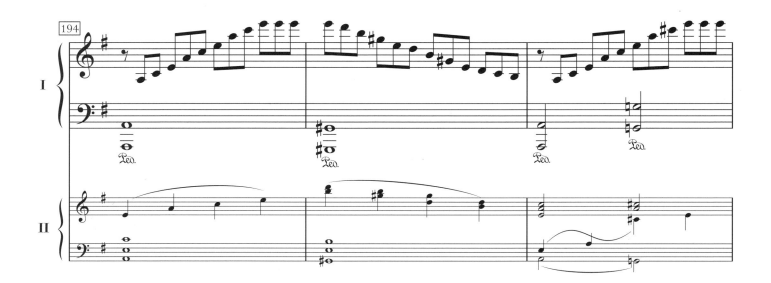

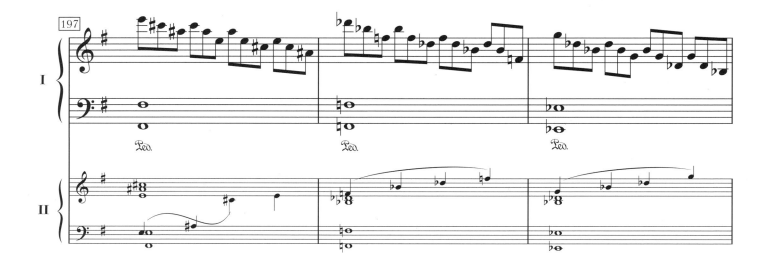

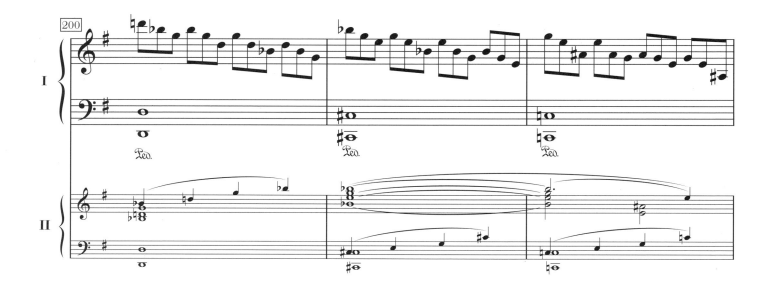

21

MMO 3085

Bar 217-218: Most people play E-natural in the bass at 217 and switch to E-flat in 218, in conformity with the orchestral part. I agree that it sounds good this way.

Bar 257-259: Many pianists do this passage with two hands (see Claude Frank). For me, it isn't hard to play it accurately with one hand and is musically and visually more in keeping with the character of the passage to do it the "hard" way.

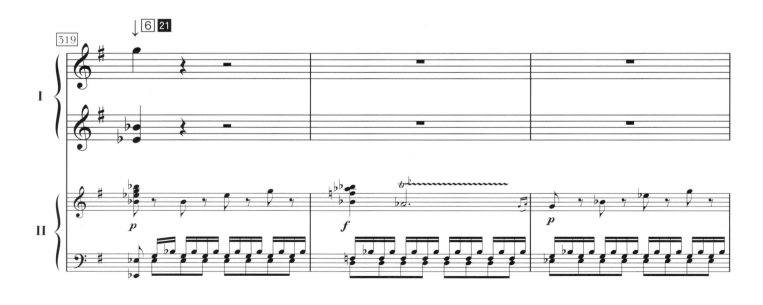

Cadenza by W.A. Mozart

Con Pedale

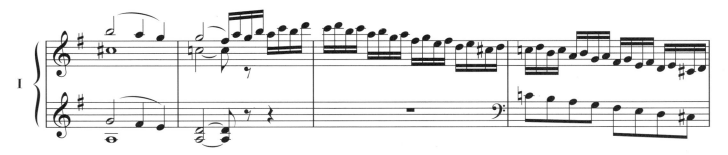

Cadenza: This, perhaps, is where some would argue against my interpretation of the trill sign in the theme at 75. Well, he wrote the suffix in here as a variant of the theme, in my opinion. Just a little nicety. I prefer this cadenza to Mozart's other one. Some mix the two for variety. Why not compose your own? It is great fun to do and a good learning experience. When you do you will discover, as I did, just how good Mozart was at being Mozart! It all sounds so obvious, clear and simple. Good luck!

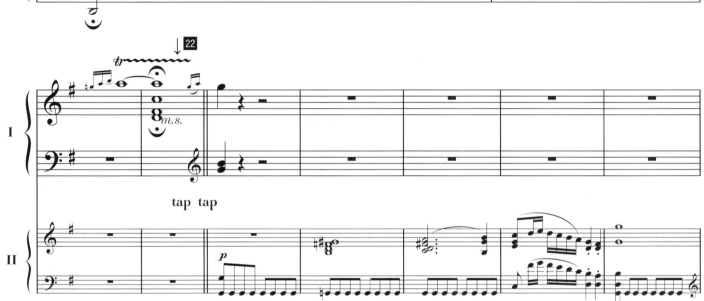

II.

Bar 35: The turn contains a c# according to Eulenberg, but this is omitted in Peters. In my view, the c natural noticeably darkens the tone of the theme. It is a matter of musical choice, but I do not see a reason why c# is called for.

tap

Pedale

Bar 66: The bassoon part needs correction in the score if you play with orchestra. Bar 73: The turn is not in the score, but really sounds musically correct.

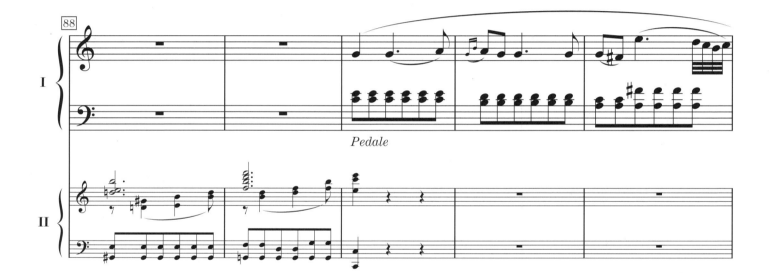

Bar 89: The orchestra should diminuendo and the piano must enter with full tone for this to work. Needs rehearsal.

Bar 99: The turn is questionably located. Some artists play it as though it were over the G, others after, as in Peters (T.A. Johnson ed.).

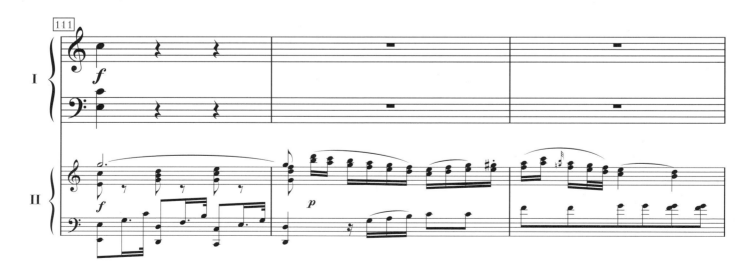

Bar 110: The turn sounds convincing with an F# despite the F in the bass. On the other hand, it is not marked.

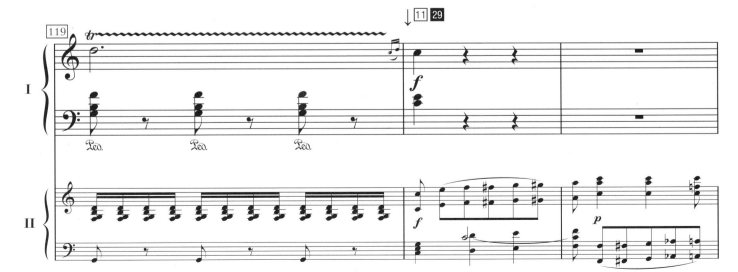

Cadenza by W.A. Mozart

Con Pedale

Con Pedale

Ped.

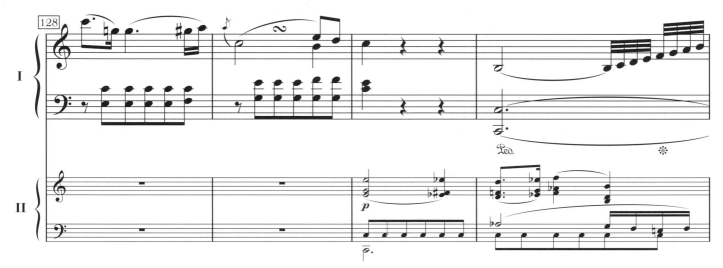

III.

Bar 16: Pick-up notes to 17 do not have a slur in the score.

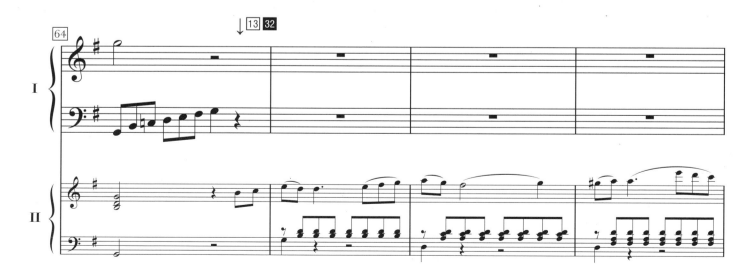

Bar 65: poco meno mosso? But only *poco!*

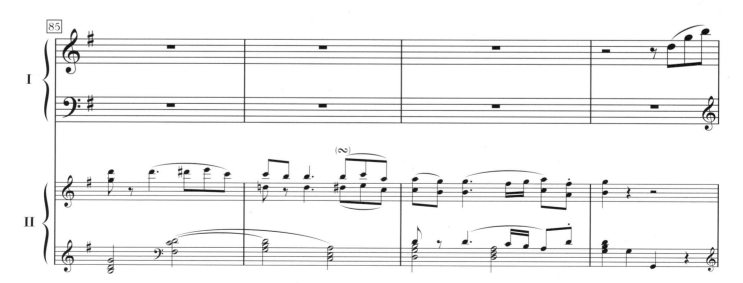

Bar 79: T.A. Johnson in his edition places a sharp sign next to the high C at beat three. The score says C natural and most performers follow the score. Frankly, I find the C natural sounds just plain wrong! Bar 78 is already full of C sharps and my ear wants the sharp here. Use your own judgment, but if your heart says C sharp, go for it!

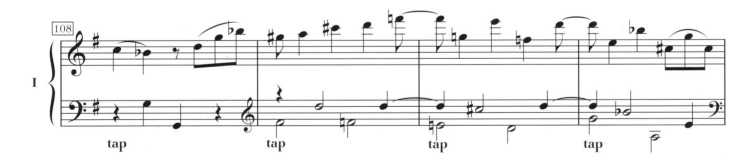

Bar 128: I have tried this connection several ways. Now, I feel it best just to complete the piano part nicely, listen for a little breathing space; (silence) and then the orchestra enters with vigor. See Claude Frank's video for other ideas:

56

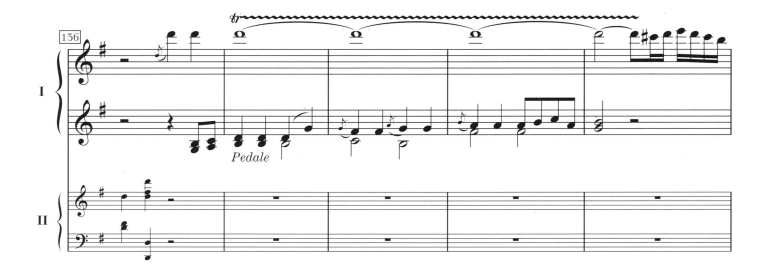

Bar 136, etc.: I believe that it is important to trust Mozart here and, while playing with really alert rhythm and touch, not to push ahead the tempo as is commonly done. At 152-156, don't worry if it feels a little static at first, just play crisply and joyfully and it will work!

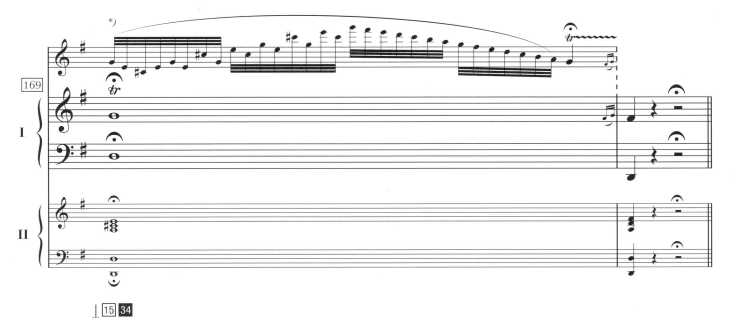

*)suggestion from Paul Van Ness

Bar 169: I like to put a little flourish here, sometimes this, sometimes that! It must be short and get back to the trill. The trill alone feels pretty dull to me. Have some fun, but be tasteful.

Bar 171- Finale, presto: This must take off, but there are a few little places which will not sound if you go as fast as you can at the beginning. Half note=76-80 is plenty fast, but not one bit slower, please!

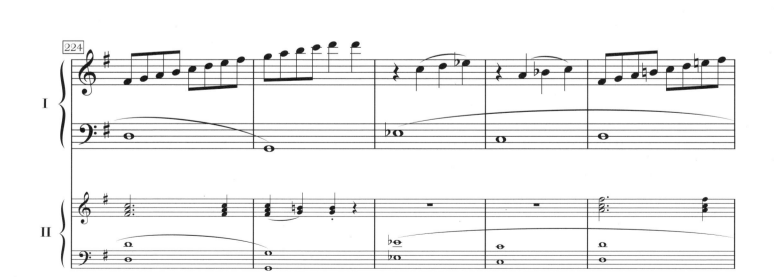

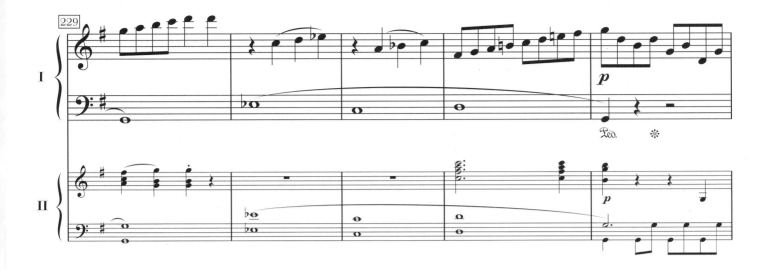

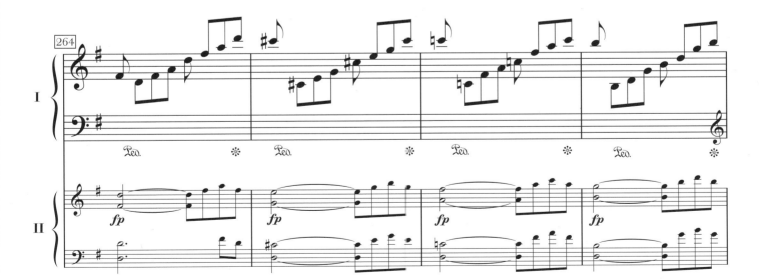

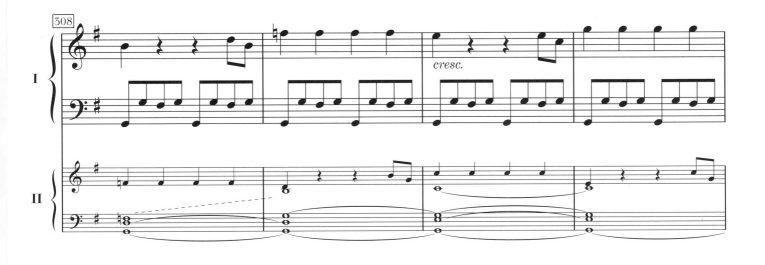

Engraving: Wieslaw Novak

MMO 3085

MUSIC MINUS ONE
50 Executive Boulevard
Elmsford, New York 10523-1325
1.800.669.7464 (U.S.)/914.592.1188 (International)

www.musicminusone.com
e-mail: mmogroup@musicminusone.com